Hal Lindsey

THE GUILT TRIP

A Barbour Book

ISBN 1-55748-740-5

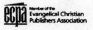

Member of the
Evangelical Christian
Publishers Association

Published by Barbour and Company, Inc.
          P.O. Box 719
          Uhrichsville, Ohio 44683

Printed in the United States of America.

The Guilt Trip

"I, even I, am the one who wipes out your transgressions for My own sake; And I will not remember your sins."
THE LORD, ISAIAH 43:25

If you were the captain of an invading army, you would find the weakest spot in your opponent's defenses and go in for the kill.

Satan, the archenemy of the saints, has a way of wiping Christians out—over and over again. He moves in on our blind side and steers us in the direction he wants.

When a person becomes a true believer in Christ, he is born into the family of God and out of the family of Satan. Satan does everything he can to keep us blinded to the offer of forgiveness in Christ, but millions have thrown off his shackles and gone from death to life. This has absolutely infuriated Satan, and each time someone responds to the Gospel, it's a slap in his

THE GUILT TRIP

face. C. S. Lewis, in his amusing book *The Screwtape Letters*, satirizes the daily routine in hell and the foibles and headaches of hardworking demons who just try to put in an honest day's work fouling up Christians.

One of the most successful tactics the demons used in neutralizing their enemies (the Christians) was to get them to dwell on all of their failures. Once they began feeling guilty about their performance in the Christian life, they were no longer any threat to Satan's program.

Things haven't changed much in Satan's tactics. Why should they? He's got a winner.

There's nothing Satan likes better than to get a believer started on the guilt trip.

As I look back over my own life, I realize that guilt is a handle that the Devil constantly tries to grab to steer me. One classic illustration that comes to mind happened to me my third year in seminary. One fellow was a real close buddy of mine. We had had three years of great times together. Then I borrowed some money from him. I told him I would be able to pay him back in about two weeks.

After a week went by, I began to be concerned a little about where the money was going to come from to pay him. But I had another week to work on it, so I wasn't too worried.

The second week went by, and I just couldn't raise the money anywhere. I felt kind of strained around my friend, but I didn't bring the subject up because I'd hoped he'd forgotten what the date was.

As the days went by, it seemed to me as though he was looking at me with an accusing expression every time I saw him, and I did the best I could to stay out of his way. After the deadline had passed by two weeks, I began planning my day so I wouldn't run into him. It was awful. I felt terrible to have lost such a good friend, but on the other hand, I couldn't see why he wasn't more understanding of my problem. Mind you, not a word had passed between us regarding the money, but I felt so guilty that I was sure he had written me off as a friend.

THE GUILT TRIP
6 - - - - - -

Finally one day, to my horror, I saw him coming toward me in the hall. There was no place to hide! He cornered me and said, "Okay, Hal, what's the matter with you?"

"Well, it's about that money I owe you," I answered defensively.

He laughed and put his big hand on my shoulder and said, "Brother, I thought that was it. Look, Hal, I haven't changed. I don't feel any different toward you than I did a few weeks ago. If you had the money, I know you'd pay me. But money doesn't mean that much to me. Your friendship means a lot more, and I'm still your buddy."

For three weeks I had been going around thinking he was condemning me. But that wasn't true at all-he was still my best friend.

That taught me an unforgettable lesson. If we think someone is holding something against us, we become alienated and hostile toward them. It's simply an inevitable reaction, a defense mechanism.

I believe this is the number one reason why

Christians fail in their relationship with God. Because we're always aware that in many ways we fall short of what we should be as Christians, it's only natural to assume that God must be displeased with our performance. The more we let God down, the more we assume His anger, until such alienation sets into our minds that it is virtually impossible for us to enjoy a vital fellowship with God.

And the pitiful tragedy is that all this is just in our minds. God isn't mad at us!

I know what some of you are thinking. You can hardly believe that what I'm saying is true. On the human level if we let people down or offend them, it does produce alienation on their part. And besides, if you've been riddled with guilt, then you have a gnawing suspicion that you really deserve God's hostility.

I want to say something loud and clear, in no uncertain terms: "He has now reconciled you in His fleshly body, through death, in order to present you before Him holy and blameless and beyond reproach—" (Colossians 1:22).

THE GUILT TRIP
8 - - - - - -

When do you become "holy and blameless and beyond reproach?" The minute He reconciles you to the Father, and that happens the moment you believe in Christ's substitutionary death on your behalf.

Let's substantiate this from the Scripture.

There are several words in the original Greek New Testament for reconciliation. One is found in Matthew 5:24: *"diallasso,"* which means that two parties are at enmity with each other and need to be reconciled by removing the cause of the enmity. This word is used strictly of human relationships in the Bible.

There is another word, however, which is always used in connection with God and man: *"apokatallasso,"* meaning that only one party has enmity in his heart and needs to have the barriers separating fellowship removed, while the other party has no enmity. You see, God has no hostility toward us. He has always loved man. This is why He became a man, so that as our substitute He could bear the judgment due us and in so doing remove every barrier that our sin had erected between Himself and us. God never needed to be reconciled; man is the one who needs it.

As the Scripture puts it, ". . . God was in Christ reconciling the world to Himself, not counting their trespasses against them . . . ," for "He made Him who knew no sin to be sin on our behalf, that we might become the righteousness of God in Him" (2 Corinthians 5 :19, 21) .

It doesn't seem like an even exchange; He gets our sin and we get His righteousness. But there you have it. It was God's incomparable plan to reconcile man back into fellowship with Him.

This is why God can say in effect to all who receive Christ, "You are *now* holy and blameless *in my sight*" (Colossians1:22; Ephesians 1:4).

Can you think of another human being, including yourself, who views you as totally holy and blameless? I can't! Yet, in God's eyes we are already perfect; not will be, but *are!*

This is not a status which is given on a temporary basis while we try to become worthy of it as Christians. Once God puts us into union with His Son, we become clothed with His righteousness and God sees us as holy and blameless because that's the way He views Jesus. Experientially we may be quite imperfect, but our acceptance in God's eyes is never based on how we perform, but rather on the fact that we are *in* Christ and God accepts Him perfectly.

Knowing these liberating facts and counting them true on a moment-by-moment basis is the most important factor in living a life pleasing to God. You can't help but respond with love and obedience to someone who loves and accepts you.

Now Satan is dedicated to keeping Christians from finding out what I've just told you, and he's done a pretty good job in the Christian world today. He lets them have a little taste of victorious living and then he moves in on them with his heavy artillery. He'll get them to fail God and get their eyes on themselves. After a series of failures, Satan gets them into a pattern that I have called "the sin syndrome."

The Sin Syndrome

First, we knowingly *sin*. The inevitable result, if we don't relate the sin to the Cross, is that we develop *guilt*. And guilt always leads to *estrangement*. There's the syndrome: *sin, guilt, estrangement*.

Now man can't live with guilt. So he tries to deal with guilt in one of two ways—both of them wrong.

If he is the type who doesn't have a particularly sensitive conscience, he tries to *justify* himself. He makes excuses and offers valid reasons why he did something:

"It was only a little lie, and it was easier on everyone involved."

"After all, the government spends my tax money on things I don't agree with anyway."

"But we really love each other, and everyone is doing it."

When we justify our actions, the result will be a feeling of loss of fellowship with God, because deep down inside we know that we haven't been honest with ourselves or God. We sense we've offended God by our deviousness. And when we feel that God has been offended, then we will also feel estranged from God. Remember, God isn't mad, but we think He is.

Another way man deals with guilt, and it's equally wrong, is to *condemn* himself. He sins over and over in the same area, guilt sets in, and then he begins the self-condemnation trip.

Satan loves to get his hands on one of these "sensitive" Christians. With no trouble at all, he can get them to feel like no-good worms before God. He'll convince them they couldn't possibly expect God to hear them when they pray, and surely He wouldn't answer their prayers even if He did hear. He gets their eyes so focused on their shabby Christian lives that they're sure God couldn't possibly use them.

Satan just sits back and relaxes when he gets us going on self-condemnation. We're out of the ball game as far as he's concerned.

At this point you may ask, is there any kind of bona fide guilt in the life of a believer in Christ?

There is what I call *"legal"* guilt. This is every man's curse as he comes into the world. It is his inherited culpability for sin, and this is what Christ removed as a barrier between God and man when He went to the cross for us. I have a lot more to say about this a little later.

Then there is the *"emotion"* of guilt. This is what Satan delights in heaping upon believers who feel they have failed God. This kind of guilt is Satan's tool and has no place in the life of a child of God.

Finally, there is a convicting ministry of the Holy Spirit described by the Apostle Paul in Second Corinthians 7:8-9 as *"sorrow"* which leads to repentance. If the "godly sorrow" caused by the Spirit's conviction doesn't lead to a repentance, or a turning around, then it well may go into the second kind of guilt, the *emotion of guilt,* which is deadly to a Christian's walk with God.

There is a need to acknowledge to God when we are guilty of sinning, and we freely can if we know for sure that God will keep on loving and accepting us. When we continue to feel unforgiven after we have acknowledged or confessed our sin, it's an indication that we have turned our focus away from God's forgiveness to ourselves. Then we're saying that our sinful weaknesses are more powerful than God's forgiving power. Either He isn't big enough to forgive us or He doesn't want to forgive us.

In either case, when there is unresolved guilt in the life of a person, he will feel estranged from God. He will not trust God to work in his life through the Holy Spirit and deliver him from the temptations of the flesh and the cunning wiles of Satan. He just won't come to God for help if he believes He is angry with him.

A Christian caught in the guilt trip will begin to seek to do things for God in the energy of the flesh to appease Him for his sense of guilt. This results in more frustration because, as the Bible says, ". . . the mind set on the flesh is hostile toward God; for it does not subject itself to the Law of God, for it is not even able to do so" (Romans 8:7).

King David of Israel certainly understood this progression. He knew quite a bit about sinning and its repercussions. Not only was he guilty of adultery with another man's wife, Bathsheba, but later he plotted her husband's death to cover up his sin.

In his later life David wrote Psalm 130, which shows us what he had learned from his rugged experiences. Listen to this particularly: "If Thou, Lord, shouldst mark iniquities, O Lord, who could stand? But there is forgiveness with Thee, that Thou mayest be feared" (Psalm 130:3-4).

In the original Hebrew the word "mark" meant to keep an itemized account of something—to write it out. David is saying here, "Lord, if You were a celestial bookkeeper keeping an itemized account of my sins, I'd be in big trouble!"

What did David learn from God's dealings with him? He learned that "there is forgiveness with (God) that (He) may be feared." That word "fear" in Hebrew means to be able to *reverently trust* someone.

David put his finger on a fantastic truth here, one of the most important things we can ever know about God. If we think God is keeping an itemized account of our sins and holding them against us, we can't really trust Him; it's impossible to have a dynamic, bold faith in Him. Why? Because you can only trust someone whom you believe really loves and accepts you *completely* in spite of all your faults.

Learning what Christ accomplished at the cross is the most important truth you will ever absorb in your lifetime. It should saturate your mind every day.

Counting as true the absolute forgiveness which Christ accomplished at the cross is the foundation of having a power-packed faith. You can't really respond to God in faith unless you know He has accepted you just as you are, unless you know what it means to be accepted in the Beloved (Ephesians 1:6). *The Beloved* is the title for God's dear Son, Jesus. God sees us all wrapped up in Jesus. The acceptance He has for

Him, the Son of His love, the Beloved One, is the acceptance He keeps on having for us.

To fail to be accepted completely by God for even one second would mean that somehow we had gotten out of Christ, and that just isn't possible. He won't let go of us! Isn't that great news?

Satan Blinds Us to the Cross

Satan would like to blind us to all this wonderful truth. In fact, he keeps trying to blind us every day. We may not even realize it, but the number one reason the power of God is short-circuited in our lives is that we have never really learned what the cross of Christ means on a day-by-day basis. The cross is the continuing basis of God accepting and forgiving us.

We've all had experiences that we consider "mountaintoppers"—times when we experienced the Holy Spirit's working in our lives in a fresh way. For a while everything was going great and then, without even really knowing why, things began to drag. Spiritual flabbiness began to weaken us, and we wondered what was wrong.

I've gone down this painful road before, and each time I've discovered the real problem: I've started of on a "guilt trip." I've failed to believe that from God's perspective I'm already forgiven for disappointing Him; I only need to claim a forgiveness that is already a fact, not beg God as if forgiveness were in doubt.

The Believer's Defense Attorney

It's the Lord's desire that His children live godly lives and not sin, but our omniscient Father, knowing our nature, made provision for His erring children.

The Apostle John, in writing to the new believers of his day, said, "My little children, I am writing these things to you that you may not sin. And if any one sins, we have an Advocate with the Father, Jesus Christ the righteous; and He Himself is the propitiation for our sins; and not for ours only, but also for those of the whole world" (1 John 2 :1-2).

An advocate means a defense attorney. Why would we need a defense attorney in the presence of God, our Father? Most of us think that it means Jesus defends us against the Father so that He won't judge us. Is that true? Absolutely not. Because of what Jesus did at the cross, the Father will never condemn us again.

The word "propitiation" means to turn away deserved wrath by the satisfaction of justice. What Christ did on the cross was to bear the compounded wrath of a Holy God on every sin that would ever be committed by every man who would ever live. The big theological word "propitiation" simply means, "God isn't mad at me anymore."

He poured out all His anger that He would have against our sins onto Jesus as He hung on the cross. Now he has set Himself free on a perfectly just basis to keep on dealing with us in love, even when He disciplines us.

God Doesn't Get Even

Are you ready for this?

God does not punish. Punishment means to "get even," and God doesn't do that. He's already "gotten even" with Jesus for all our sins. God "disciplines" His children, but it's always in love—never in anger. The words "discipline" and "training" are interchangeable words. God's disciplining always has a forward look to it (Hebrews 12:5-13).

When God sees a child of His who continually refuses to depend upon the Holy Spirit to deliver him from his temptations, then out of deep concern for that child's well-being and happiness God will begin to train him so that he will come to depend upon Him in the future. God knows we are only happy when we are living holy lives. This is true discipline and it has no resemblance to punishment.

Sometimes this discipline may seem grievous, but if we are learning to see everything that comes our way as being permitted by the loving hand of our Heavenly Father, then we can give thanks even for the discipline.

Unfortunately, at this point Satan has taken his toll with many believers. They live in constant fear of punishment for their sins.

Most of us have a few especially gross sins we committed in our past that spook us like the proverbial skeleton in the closet. Whenever some difficulty or calamity hits our lives, we trot the skeleton out and say, "Oh yes, God is getting even with me for 'that sin'."

Some live with the gnawing fear that lightning is going to strike them or God is going to kill one of their children to get even with them for some sin they committed long ago or are involved in at the moment.

God does not deal with us that way. To be sure, adversities are permitted in the believer's life, but they are designed to teach us to trust God, not to destroy us with vengeance.

But What About. . .

Now some of you may be saying, "All right, Hal, if God never punishes us for our sins, what about Galatians 6:7 which says, 'Do not be deceived, God is not mocked; for whatever a man sows, this he will also reap'?"

This verse is jerked out of context by so many Christians that it's incredible. The verse just before this one says, "And let the one who is taught the Word share all good things with him who teaches" (Galatians 6:6). This context is talking about supporting financially the one who gives himself to studying and teaching the Bible.

This same idea of sowing money for God's work is contained in Second Corinthians 9:6,

"Now this I say, he who *sows* sparingly shall also reap sparingly; and he who sows bountifully shall also reap bountifully.

This concept of "whatsoever a man sows, he shall also reap" is concerned with investing our money in God's work and the reward or lack of reward for our stewardship.

To apply this passage to God's method of discipline is to contradict the whole principle of grace with which God now deals with His children.

Satan, the Old Guilt Tripper

If you still feel guilty after you acknowledge your sin and have remembered that you are forgiven, guess who is laying it on you. It's the old guilt-tripper himself, Satan.

Satan does not want you to remember that God did away with your sin at the cross. That's why you need a defense attorney before the Father. Satan's name means "The Accuser."

Christ doesn't have to defend you against the Father; He defends you against Satan, before the Father.

Here's a scene which has probably taken place in heaven in the presence of God today. We can thank Job for this bit of insight into Satan's tactics.

Satan's been up there today with a portfolio on each one of God's children. He brought a dossier on Buzz and Tom and Karin and an especially large file on Hal. He charges in and points, "Ah ha! There's Hal. He's one of Your children, huh? Did you see what he just did?"

And Satan begins to accuse.

Then Jesus steps up and says, "Father, Hal believed in Me in 1956. The forgiveness I paid for at the cross was then applied to him. This is our only plea."

And the Father says, "Case dismissed!"

God will not let anyone discipline His children but Himself. He'll do it in love because He has set Himself free to deal with us in grace. God, on the basis of His indwelling Spirit whom He trusts and has put into the life of every believer, is conforming us daily into the image of Jesus.

Old Testament Pictures

There's a wonderful picture in the Old Testament of Christ's intercessory work for believers. He bears our names upon His heart as He continually represents us before the Father.

We're taught this in the Old Testament from the practice of the high priest. He would go into the Tabernacle before the Presence of the Lord, before the Ark, as it was called, and he would burn incense, which was a picture of prayer.

Bound over his heart was a special vest with precious stones upon it, and on each stone were the names of the children of Israel.

God said, "And Aaron shall carry the names of the sons of Israel . . . over his heart when he enters the holy place, for a memorial before the Lord continually" (Exodus 28:29).

This is a beautiful picture of how Jesus Christ continually is before the throne of God with your name on His heart.

That's why in Hebrews 7:24-25 we have these encouraging words: "but He, on the other hand, because He abides forever, holds His priesthood permanently. Hence also He is able to save forever those who draw near to God through Him, since He always lives to make intercession for them."

According to this fantastic promise of assurance, once we have believed in Christ as Savior, it is impossible to be lost again or unforgiven. For a child of God to become lost, Christ would have to stop interceding for him. The promise is that "He is able to save *forever* those who draw near to God through Him. "Forever" is a very long time.

Jesus Himself promised, "I will never desert you, nor will I ever forsake you" (Hebrews 13:5). Thank God that "He always lives to make intercession for us," and because of that we can "draw near with confidence to the throne of grace, that we may receive mercy and find grace to help in time of need" (Hebrews 4:16).

Satan: Accuser Before God and Conscience

After Satan accuses us before God and doesn't make any headway there, he begins to accuse our consciences. He'll get us into a hopeless treadmill: sinning, vowing we won't do it again, trying not to sin, and then sinning again.

Here's the way it works:

First, he'll start working on an area of weakness. Every Christian has at least one area where he is especially vulnerable. We still have the old sin nature in us which can tempt us, and when we don't depend upon the indwelling Holy Spirit to overcome temptations, we will sin.

Seeking to be a good Christian we might say, "God, I know I've been wrong: thank you for forgiving me." Our burden is lifted and everything goes along fine for awhile. Then Satan gets us to fall down again in the same area. We hate ourselves for being such an awful Christian, but we accept His forgiveness and keep moving—only we're feeling a little guilty about having so little will power to live for God.

Pretty soon Satan will get us to sin again in the same area, and this time we're feeling so unworthy that we promise, "Oh God, if You'll just forgive me one more time, I vow I won't do this again."

At this piece of news, Satan and his demon hordes let out a rousing cheer of victory. He has us right where he wants us—on the sin treadmill.

We try so hard to please God, only we do it in the power of the flesh. The harder we try, the more we fail. The more we fail, the more we vow not to do it again.

Then Satan steps in and says accusingly, "Too bad! God won't forgive you this time. You've had it. There's no more grace for you."

Or if he sees that we're too smart to fall for that extreme line of reasoning, he'll say, "God may forgive you, but He can't forget how unreliable you are. You'll never be able to be used by God as fully as before."

It's that old "bird with the broken wing will never fly so high again" routine.

Wham! You're wiped out! You forget that the issue is not *will* God forgive you, but will you believe that He *has* forgiven you and trust Him for the inner strengthening to turn from sin.

I'm not trying to teach that we can go out and sin and have no conscience about it, so don't get all up-tight about that. The Holy Spirit will faithfully convict a believer of sin, not so he can confess in order to get forgiven, but so that he can claim forgiveness and believe Him again.

God does not want us to dwell on our sins, but rather on our forgiveness. If your focus is continually on yourself, then you cannot be "Looking away [from all that will distract] to Jesus" (Hebrews 12:2, *Amplified Bible*).

When you finally understand what Jesus

Christ accomplished at the cross, you realize that God never stops forgiving you, even while you're in the process of sinning, although you yourself cannot appreciate the comfort of the forgiveness while you're sinning.

When Christ died on the cross, how many of your sins were future? Every last one of them.

I used to think that when I accepted Christ it meant that Christ had died for my sins up to that point, but from that point on I'd just have to confess them as I did them or else I wasn't forgiven. That's a perilous position to be in because you're never quite sure if you've confessed all your sins, and there just might be one or two that God is holding against you.

One day I realized what the *all* in Colossians 2:13 meant: "And when you were dead in your transgressions and the uncircumcision of your flesh, He made you alive together with Him, having forgiven us *all* our transgressions."

We were dead before we accepted Jesus, dead spiritually, unable to know God as a living reality, as a Person.

Then the Bible says, "He made you *alive* together with Him." This is talking about the new birth, the experience of being given spiritual life the moment you believe in Christ. Why is this possible? "Having forgiven us *all* our transgressions."

The verb translated "having forgiven" means something which happens at a point of time that doesn't have to be repeated. A final act. In God's mind, how many does that *all* mean? How many of our sins did God see when He judged them in Jesus on the cross?

The answer is *all!*

God Sees the Whole Parade of Life

God is looking at our lives as a helicopter pilot would look down at a parade. If we're standing on a corner watching a parade, we see the beginning of the parade, each segment passing by, and then we see the end of it. We see consecutively. But God, like the pilot, sees the whole parade at one time. That's the way God sees your life: your past, present, and future is all in the *now* with Him.

When you place faith in Jesus as your Savior, God has already seen (back in A.D. 33) your life go by like a parade. He took your whole life and the sin and guilt of it and put it all on Jesus Christ.

So when you believe in Christ as Savior, how many sins has God forgiven you? Not just those you have committed up to that point, but those from your whole lifetime. He couldn't accept you into a relationship with Himself at all unless He could forgive you for the whole thing.

This doesn't mean that God condones sinning in the life of a believer—far from it. It means He has set Himself free to be ready to work in us the moment we see that we've sinned and acknowledge it and accept His forgiveness.

First John 1:9 says, "If we keep on confessing our sins, He is faithful and righteous, to have forgiven us our sins and to have cleansed us

from all un-righteousness" (literal translation of
the Greek verb tenses). The Word never tells a
believer *after the cross* to ask forgiveness. It's
already a settled fact with God, and He just
wants us to claim what is already true.

In First John 1:9 the word "confess" means
to agree with someone about something; in this
case to agree with God about our sins. But I
can't agree with God about His attitude toward
my sins until I see clearly what His attitude is.

Agree with God

First of all, God wants us to see our sin as He
sees it—it is sin. But He doesn't want us to stop
there. If we really agree with God about our sin,
then we also have to see it as already forgiven.
That's the way God sees it. Finally, He wants us
to turn from the sin and begin to trust Him to
empower us to have victory over it in the future.

If we don't judge our sin in this way, accepting His forgiveness and turning from the sin in

His power, Satan is going to come in and grab hold of that handle of guilt. He will get us to try to make up for our sins, and we'll end up punishing ourselves or someone else to try to relieve the guilt

Someone Has to Pay

Every time we sin, we instinctively know someone has to pay for it. We don't have to be taught that; it's part of our very make-up. When I sin, either I've got to pay for it, or I make someone else pay (usually those dearest to me), or I look to Jesus as already having paid for it.

In the years I have been a believer I have had many counseling experiences in this area. I remember a beautiful young girl whose husband had to go on a long trip abroad. While he was gone, she committed adultery. That was a sin, no question about it.

After this happened she realized it was a sin and acknowledged this to God. But she didn't

believe what God said, that it was already forgiven. She did not count His forgiveness as being
true in her case. She was in much worse shape
than she realized, because unresolved guilt is one
of the most destructive forces on earth.

Her husband returned. Deeply implanted in
that girl's mind was the sin and the unresolved
guilt from it—not because God still held her
guilty, but because she didn't believe what God
said and therefore she didn't forgive herself.

A few years after her husband returned, they
had their first child. Satan began to put his hand
into her subconscious mind and grab hold of
that guilt. Pretty soon she was having serious
mental problems. She told her husband what had
happened, thinking that maybe this would clear
her conscience. He forgave her, but she still
couldn't forgive herself.

Do you know what she wound up doing?
One day her husband came in and found her trying to strangle their child. Why? Because she
loved that child more than anything in the world.
Killing him was a way of inflicting maximum

punishment upon herself for the sense of guilt. What a needless tragedy!

She didn't understand all this at first until it was unraveled in counseling. Deep down inside was this unresolved guilt. Instead of relating this to the cross of Jesus Christ and saying, "Thank You for forgiving me," she had tried to punish herself for what she had done. She instinctively knew that someone had to pay, and she was making herself pay.

Guilt is the most crippling disease in the world today!

A friend of mine was in a doctor's office when he looked across the street at a hotel and saw a woman about ready to jump from the tenth floor. He rushed across the street, went up in the elevator, and got there just in time to say, "Wait, don't jump. Let me just talk to you."

Slowly and distinctively he said, "God loves you."

The girl turned and looked at him with a horrible expression of guilt and despair, then turned and jumped. She was killed immediately.

Psychiatrists and doctors say that un-resolved guilt is the number one cause of mental illness and suicide. Over half of all hospital beds are filled with people who have emotional ill-nesses. The greatest therapy they could possibly have would be to find out that God loves them and has made an all-encompassing forgiveness available to them in Christ.

God didn't have to wait until Freud came along to have an answer for mental illness. We don't have to go to a psychiatrist to get the answer for guilt. Jesus provided the only real answer to guilt some two thousand years ago. If we believe what God has said, there's an answer that cleanses us in our conscience and sets us free from dead works to serve the living God.

I don't want you to suffer from crippling guilt like this. I want you to be able to release the power of God in your life day by day, moment by moment-to be set free from a guilt complex and be able to acknowledge to God, "Yes, Lord, I'm guilty, but I thank You that I've been forgiven."

Then turn and believe that the Spirit of God

will work in your life right now. You don't have to wait until you are worthy of it or earn it.

Here's a passage that thrills me every time I read it—it never gets old. "Having canceled out the certificate of debt, consisting of decrees against us and which was hostile to us; and He has taken it out of the way, having nailed it to the cross" (Colossians 2:14).

Out of Debt

This is a powerful word picture. In the day in which this was written the word translated as "certificate of debt" was widely known. Whenever a person would be convicted in a Roman court, a "certificate of debt" or bond would be prepared. The scribe of the court would itemize and write down every crime for which the person had been convicted. This certificate meant that the prisoner owed Caesar a prescribed payment for those crimes. It would then be taken with the prisoner to wherever he would be imprisoned and nailed to the door of his cell.

What an illustration the Apostle Paul used to show how God has dealt with our sins. When Jesus hung on the cross nineteen centuries ago, the "certificate of debt" of every man who would ever live was nailed to the cross with Him.

Our certificate of debt lists every time that we fall short of God's perfect law in thought, word, or deed. Just as that certificate would have been nailed to the cell of the criminal, Jesus took our certificate of debt and nailed it to the cross.

Why? Because He intended to pay for it.

According to Roman law, when a person was put in prison and the certificate of debt was nailed to the door, it would remain there until the sentence was carried out. Then they would take this certificate and write across it the word meaning "It is finished." They would roll it up, give it to the prisoner, and he could never be punished for those crimes again.

Did you know that was one of the last things Jesus shouted from the cross?

Just before He bowed His head and said,

"Father, into Your hands I commit my spirit," He gave a cry of victory. He called from the cross "It is finished." The Greek word for this is "tetelestai," meaning "paid in full" (John 19:30).

Paid in Full

Jesus took our certificate of debt and wrote across it in His own blood, "Paid in full." We can never be tried for our sins again after we receive the pardon. It's settled forever in heaven by the blood of the only begotten Son of God.

That's why it says in Colossians 2:14, "He has taken it (our certificate of debt) out of the way, having nailed it to the cross." I owe God perfect obedience to His law, but God will never grade my law-keeping on the curve. It's perfection or nothing—and I can't pay.

That's what the word "redemption" means: to purchase out of slavery and set free by paying the price of a ransom. The ransom that Christ had to pay to set us free was the price of our owing God perfect obedience to His law, and Christ paid the sentence of debt in full. "...knowing that you were not redeemed with perishable things like silver or gold from your futile way of life inherited from your forefathers, but with precious blood, as of a lamb unblemished and spotless, the blood of Christ" (1 Peter 1:18-19).

That's why it says in Colossians 2:15: "When He had disarmed the rulers and authorities, He made a public display of them, having triumphed over them through Him."

The "rulers and authorities" are Satan and all his armies.

And Christ disarmed them! They have no legal basis to put their hands on a child of God any more. *Satan has no legal grounds to work in a Christian's life.* We can give him the legal ground, if we don't want to believe in God, but we certainly don't have to. God wants us to take our Magna Charta of freedom, which is the perfect forgiveness of Jesus Christ, and to realize that when we sin we should come to Him immediately with the heart attitude, "Oh, Lord,

I agree with You that I have sinned." This is not in order to be forgiven, however. It's just to realize a forgiveness which is already a fact.

When Christ died on the cross, He took care of the sin problem forever. Another sacrifice will never be necessary. Why? Because of the value of the life of the One who was sacrificed. It's not like the blood of the goats and the bulls in the Old Testament, which merely covered sin. When Christ died for sin, He took it away as an issue.

"And not through the blood of goats and calves, but through His own blood, He entered the holy place once for all, *having obtained eternal redemption*" (Hebrews 9:12).

How long is eternal? God doesn't offer anything less. It is based upon the value of the sacrifice of Jesus Christ.

"For if the blood of goats and bulls and the ashes of a heifer sprinkling those who have been defiled, sanctify for the cleansing of the flesh, how much more will the blood of Christ, who through the eternal Spirit offered Himself without blemish to God, *cleanse your conscience*

from dead works to serve the living God?"
(Hebrews 9:13-14).

License to Serve

This is the most powerful message the Holy Spirit ever brought home to me. It was a license to serve, not to sin. The motivation which comes from knowing a perfect acceptance with God is so much greater than walking in fear that you're going to lose the relationship that there's just no comparison.

God wants us to serve not out of duty, but out of thanksgiving for what He has done in Jesus Christ.

"Cleanse your conscience"—that's where guilt becomes imbedded—"from dead works to serve the living God."

A "dead work" is anything which you and I do to try to help God forgive us for our sin. It is trying to add to what Christ has fully accomplished on the cross.

A dead work is when we don't believe we're really forgiven and we try to do something to make up for what we've done.

What does God want us to do when we sin?

We need Him at that moment more than at any other time in our lives. It's not a time for running from God, as Adam did. When Adam sinned, God appeared in the Garden and said, "Adam, where are you?" Did God really need to ask? Don't you think He knew where Adam was?

Adam hid himself because he was afraid. He should have known that God still loved him or He wouldn't have been looking for him. Then Adam committed the first dead work of history! He tried to hide his sense of guilt with fig leaves. He tried to cover his sin and guilt by the work of his own hands, and in doing that he committed the first "religious" act. That's really what "religion" is, if you understand it correctly.

Christianity isn't a religion; Christianity is a personal relationship with God through Jesus Christ and His finished work. It's not our trying to gain God s approbation by what we do.

In God's Family

Think of it!

We have an access into the presence of God. "Let us draw near with a sincere heart in full assurance of faith, having our hearts sprinkled clean from an evil conscience and our body washed with pure water" (Hebrews 10:22).

When we knowingly sin, God wants us to draw near to Him "with a sincere heart," to be honest "in full assurance of faith" (i.e., in what Christ has done). "By this will we have been sanctified through the offering of the body of Jesus Christ once for all" (Hebrews 10:10).

God loves us and accepts us. We're forgiven. He wants us to own up to what we've done and thank Him for His forgiveness. If we don't do this, we will have an evil conscience.

I know one heart-breaking story after another of people who have gone into mental illness because of unresolved guilt; others remain reasonably sane but have no power in their lives.

They try to draw upon some experience they have had in their past and wonder why they don't have the same power any more.

How absolutely fantastic to know there is a forgiveness which is guaranteed to us through the once-and-for-all offering of Jesus Christ on our behalf. That's why it says, "Therefore He is able also to save to the uttermost—completely, perfectly, finally and for all time and eternity—those who come to God through Him, since He is always living to make petition to God *and* intercede with Him and intervene for them" (Hebrews 7:25, *Amplified Bible*). I'm sure that some of you reading this have allowed guilt to tie you in knots for years. You've just been waiting for God to lower the boom on you for some secret sin or for a life lived in open rebellion against His will for you. That very guilt has produced an estrangement from the one Person you need to be closest to right now—your loving Heavenly Father. Can't you see how wonderful it would be to have Him fold His great, strong arms of love around you and comfort and reassure you of His love and acceptance?

Let Him do it now. He isn't angry with you—no matter how much you've let Him down. He has utterly forgiven you for any offenses toward Him. The only thing that grieves God now is for His children to feel alienated toward Him when He cares for them so much.